To...

De...
Nervi, the inter...
Tower was the world's tallest reinforced
concrete building when it opened in 1964.
800 Square Victoria

Old Montreal Ouest

Once a spookily quiet graveyard of empty
buildings, the west side of the old city is
now jumping with loft conversions and cafés,
classy bookshops and stylish restaurants.

Aldred Building

Montreal's first modern skyscraper, this 1929
deco gem calls to mind a squat Empire State
Building. Its limestone cladding helps it blend
with the older buildings on this historic square.
507 place d'Armes

Place Ville-Marie

IM Pei and Henry N Cobb's cruciform tower
is a sleek statement of the high International
Style. The bar at the top, Altitude 737 (T 514
397 0737), boasts the best view in the city.
See p012

Place Jacques-Cartier

The heart of Old Montreal is a tourist magnet
and popular venue for outdoor performances
of music and comedy during the summer.

Old Port

The former wharves on the St Lawrence have
been converted into a public space that's used
for everything from garden exhibitions to
a viewing spot for the city's annual fireworks.

Parc du Mont-Royal

The hill from which the city gets its name is
good for jogging, taking in the cityscape and
impromptu drumming on Sunday mornings.

INTRODUCTION
THE CHANGING FACE OF THE URBAN SCENE

For 100 years, Montreal was the economic powerhouse of Canada. Then, in the late 1960s and 1970s, Quebec nationalism and the Anglophone reaction to it saw businesses, wealth and jobs flee the city, as the corporate élite moved to Toronto. Endless constitutional wrangling didn't help, and the city spent almost two decades in the economic doldrums. Its appeal as a tourist destination rested largely on its proximity to the American market – a kind of Europe without the jet lag. It also had a reputation as something of a party town, dating from 1920s boozers dodging US Prohibition.

The change in the last decade has been dramatic. Montreal has rebuilt its economy on the back of creative industries such as film production, computer games and even circus skills, and it is proud of its UNESCO designation as a City of Design. Urban regeneration in the inner city has also taken the form of boutique hotels, style-led eateries and a plethora of stores offering the best in avant-garde furniture, accessories and clothes.

The city has invested heavily in arts festivals, and this approach, which has run from hosting the Gay Olympics to comedy events and fireworks competitions, has paid off. The city feels like an electric, buzzy place to be. And the thing that caused Montreal all the problems, its Francophone exceptionalism, is now its greatest strength. From its fabulous restaurants to its open approach to visitors, it supplies the best of France and the best of Canada.

ESSENTIAL INFO
FACTS, FIGURES AND USEFUL ADDRESSES

TOURIST OFFICE
Infotouriste Centre
1001 rue Square-Dorchester
T 514 873 2015
www.tourism-montreal.org

TRANSPORT
Car hire
Avis
T 514 866 2847
www.avis.com
Hertz
T 514 938 1717
www.hertz.com
Public transport
T 514 786 4636
www.stm.info
Taxis
Champlain
T 514 273 2435
Taxi Hochelaga
T 514 382 1010

EMERGENCY SERVICES
Ambulance/Fire/Police
T 911
24-hour pharmacy
Pharmaprix
5122 Côte-des-Neiges
T 514 738 8464
www.pharmaprix.ca

CONSULATES
British Consulate-General
Suite 4200
1000 rue de la Gauchetière Ouest
T 514 866 5863
www.britishembassy.gov.uk
US Consulate
1155 rue St-Alexandre
T 514 398 9695
montreal.usconsulate.gov

MONEY
American Express
3333 boulevard Cavendish
T 514 488 9910
travel.americanexpress.com

POSTAL SERVICES
Post Office
800 boulevard René-Lévesque Ouest
T 514 395 4909
Shipping
UPS
1241 avenue McGill College
T 1 800 742 5877
www.ups.com

BOOKS
Montreal: The Unknown City by Kristian
Gravenor and John David Gravenor
(Arsenal Pulp Press)
**Sacré Blues: An Unsentimental
Journey Through Quebec** by Taras
Grescoe (Macfarlane Walter & Ross)

WEBSITES
Architecture
www.cca.qc.ca
Newspaper
www.canada.com/montrealgazette

COST OF LIVING
**Taxi from Montreal-Trudeau
International Airport to Downtown**
£16
Cappuccino
£1.40
Packet of cigarettes
£4.70
Daily newspaper
£0.45
Bottle of champagne
£65

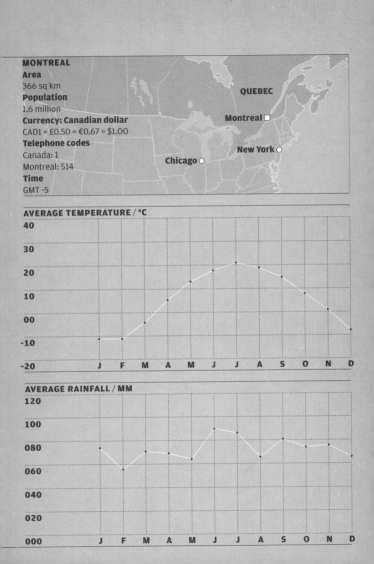

MONTREAL
Area
366 sq km
Population
1.6 million
Currency: Canadian dollar
CAD1 = £0.50 = €0.67 = $1.00
Telephone codes
Canada: 1
Montreal: 514
Time
GMT -5

QUEBEC

Montreal □

New York ○

Chicago ○

AVERAGE TEMPERATURE / °C

40
30
20
10
00
-10
-20

J F M A M J J A S O N D

AVERAGE RAINFALL / MM

120
100
080
060
040
020
000

J F M A M J J A S O N D

NEIGHBOURHOODS

THE AREAS YOU NEED TO KNOW AND WHY

To help you navigate the city, we've chosen the most interesting districts (see below and the map inside the back cover) and colour-coded our featured venues, according to their location; those venues that are outside these areas are not coloured.

PLATEAU
The eminently strollable, liveable Plateau Mont-Royal is the city's shopping, eating and drinking zone. Its chic supper clubs, such as Globe Restaurant (3455 boulevard St-Laurent, T 514 284 3823), and French cafés, such as L'Express (3927 rue St-Denis, T 514 845 5333), are a big draw.

MULTIMEDIA CITY
Just across rue McGill from Old Montreal, this former industrial enclave isn't so architecturally precious as the old city, and has seen high-tech offices carved out of existing buildings and new ones added. It's home to great cafés and galleries, and a waterfront of huge grain towers.

OUTREMONT
Sassy, Francophone and classy, avenue Laurier has long been famous for its sophisticated shopping, ladies-who-lunch and neighbourhood of upscale residences. Now a kind of coolness-creep is making its way towards Mile End and new going-out places are appearing all the time.

DOWNTOWN
A few short canyons of skyscrapers and miles of underground city for wintertime, Downtown has been given a shot in the arm by the new design-led International Quarter that reunites it with Old Montreal. At its top end, rue Sherbrooke is the city's main artery, which is home to swanky department stores and cultural institutions.

GAY VILLAGE
In a way that is unimaginable in cities south of the Canadian border, Montreal has branded its gay neighbourhood, complete with lamppost images of smiling queens and, for some reason, lots of potted palms. Come to this lively district for fun, friendship and antiques.

MILE END
When the artists and designers started to move out of Plateau, they migrated north to the Jewish district of Mile End. They were followed by boho boutiques, such as Commissaires (see p073) and Renata Morales (see p078), and cool bars, creating a new hipster 'hood.

OLD MONTREAL
Once, only the cobblestone lanes around place Jacques-Cartier were thronged with tourists. The rest of the old city was ghostly, after the flight of money to Toronto or to Downtown's office blocks. Now the western end is jumping with designer hotels, classy shops and sophisticated eateries.

LATIN QUARTER
During the summer months, the legendary open-air Montreal International Jazz Festival (www.montrealjazzfest.com), as well as the Just for Laughs comedy festival (www.justforlaughs.ca) and many other events, take over the streets of the Latin Quarter, turning its network of bars and restaurants into the city's party central.

LANDMARKS
THE SHAPE OF THE CITY SKYLINE

The first thing you have to do to get to grips with Montreal's layout is tip your head to one side and ignore a conventional approach to the compass. Although the island of Montreal is croissant-shaped, with its ends pointing south-west and north-east and the city centre in the middle, locals tilt everything so that Old Montreal is at the south of their mental map, despite really being in the west. From here, you can see Buckminster Fuller's geodesic dome (overleaf) on an island in the St Lawrence. Boulevard St-Laurent, known as The Main, runs up the middle of the city, dividing it into the traditionally Anglophone west and the Francophone east. The language divisions have been completely blurred, but the Ouest and Est divisions live on in the street addresses and numbering.

Apart from the Downtown buildings, such as IM Pei's Place Ville-Marie (see p012) and the rather stolid Sun Life Building (see p062), other major distinguishing features include Mont-Royal, which gives the city its name but is really more of a hill than a mountain, and, of course, the vast river, without which none of this would be here. Other major arteries include the culturally rich rue Sherbrooke, the tatty shopping street of rue Ste-Catherine and the more interesting rue St-Denis. In summer, much of it can be covered on foot, and in winter, the metro system can take you some of the way. All of it is safe, and taxis are not expensive.
For full addresses, see Resources.

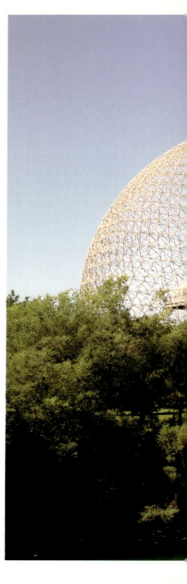

Biosphère

The most iconic structure remaining from Expo 67 is the former US pavilion designed by Richard Buckminster Fuller and Shoji Sadao. A 63m geodesic steel dome with acrylic panels, the frame was meant to be bolted together, but was welded in places. When repairs were made in 1976, a welder's torch set fire to the transparent acrylic bubble, vaporising it in 20 minutes. The dome lay empty until 1995, when a new structure was built inside to house Canada's first Ecowatch Centre, dedicated to the ecosystems of the St Lawrence and the Great Lakes. Even without its skin, which was not replaced due to heating costs, the dome is a ghostly presence on the skyline, and up close, its size and sheer power remain impressive. Sadly, the futuristic monorail that once ran through the dome is long gone.

160 chemin Tour-de-l'Isle, Île Ste-Hélène, T 514 283 5000, biosphere.ec.gc.ca

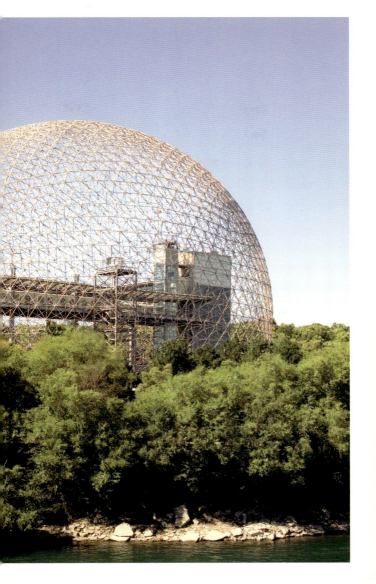

Place Ville-Marie

The construction of IM Pei and Henry N Cobb's International Style tower, which was completed in 1962, signalled the move of the city's financial heart from Old Montreal to Downtown. One of the pair's first major collaborations, it came at a time when the city and its charismatic mayor, Jean Drapeau, were garnering global attention for Montreal's ambitious architecture, particularly in the run-up to Expo 67. The low-rise buildings and open spaces around the tower are part of the same project, and when it opened, Place Ville-Marie was the world's largest and most complex office building. Complex because it connected with underground railway lines, metro lines and shopping malls, and was the epicentre of Montreal's winter-busting underground city.

1 place Ville-Marie

Atwater Market

The charming Atwater Market was built in 1933 by local church architect Ludger Lemieux, and it had space for as many as 300 merchants on the ground floor inside and out. The second-floor hall can house 10,000 people and has witnessed everything from secessionist rallies to boxing bouts. Jean Drapeau wanted the market razed in 1968, but local backlash saved it, and the city instead spent more than £500,000 refurbishing it during the 1980s. This great food market now stands as a developer's beacon, calling in a new generation of aspirational homebuyers who are keen to sniff out the next on-the-up city neighbourhood. The presence of the restaurant Joe Beef (see p040) and some natty antiques shops around the corner suggest they're on to something. *138 avenue Atwater, T 514 937 7754*

Westmount Square
Opened in 1967, the four blocks in upscale Westmount – two commercial and two residential – were designed by Mies van der Rohe's office following the success of his Seagram Building in New York. Like his Toronto-Dominion Centre and Chicago Federal Center, Westmount Square very much used the Seagram as an unadorned, muscularly corporate blueprint.
Westmount Square

HOTELS
WHERE TO STAY AND WHICH ROOMS TO BOOK

Ah, the difference a decade makes. In the late 1990s, with Quebec Province in the economic doldrums, your main hotel choices were limited to a smattering of American-chain towers scattered around the vacant lots of Downtown, and the fading attractions of <u>The Ritz-Carlton</u> (1228 rue Sherbrooke Ouest, T 514 842 4212) or <u>Fairmont The Queen Elizabeth</u> (900 boulevard René-Lévesque Ouest, T 514 861 3511). Now, there is frankly an embarrassment of choice, in what has become Canada's boutique-hotel capital. Old buildings, dating from the 17th century to the 1970s, have been reborn as chic designer destinations and sumptuous hideaways.

The key development has been the reorientating of the city's pleasure zones towards Old Montreal, which is newly reunited with Downtown by the International Quarter development that bridges a major freeway. The grand bank and trading buildings that once surveyed eerily quiet canyons of a dead financial district have, in their hotel reincarnations, been the leading forces in reinvigorating the whole neighbourhood. Many house destination bars and restaurants for Montreal's beautiful people and, in so doing, make you feel like you are part of the city, not a disembodied visitor in an anonymous pod. Best of all, virtually every hotel will seem like great value for those used to stumping up for cramped rooms in less friendly cities such as London or New York.

For full addresses and room rates, see Resources.

Sofitel

When developer David J Azrieli bulldozed the art deco Van Horne mansion in 1973 to build a dull office tower, he attracted the ire of the public and local conservationists. With his redevelopment of the block into an airy hotel for the French Sofitel chain, some forgiveness may be due. Working with architects Michelange Panzini and GSM Design, Azrieli's Sofitel dishes up art in the lobby, such as the stained-glass window (above), designed by local artists Isaac Alt and Titu Dragotesco, 3m-high ceilings and high-quality accommodation for the corporate captain. Only 16 of the 255 rooms are suites, but they have a solid, robber-baron feel. The location at the foot of Mont-Royal is hard to beat for those with both culture and capitalism in mind.
1155 rue Sherbrooke Ouest,
T 514 285 9000, www.sofitel.com

Hôtel St-Paul

When it opened in 2001, this boutique hotel was the first major business to show how Old Montreal could be rescued from decay and tourist tack. The 120-room hotel was given a warm but minimalist look by the owner's wife, designer Ana Borrallo, who included a large, alabaster-covered fireplace in the main lobby, high quantities of leather and suede, and a very Canadian sprinkling of furs. The feeling is high design without being so rarefied as to give you hotel-room alienation, thanks to the earthy palette used. Book a Deluxe Suite or the Penthouse Junior Suite 1005 (right) and indulge your royal fantasies in a bed surrounded by yards of creamy, uplit fabric. The Vauvert restaurant (T 514 876 2823) is a hot spot for both foodies and poseurs and was given a new, dark look in 2007 by Jean-Guy Chabauty of Moderno. *355 rue McGill, T 514 380 2222, www.hotelstpaul.com*

W Montreal

Arriving in September 2004, after Montreal had already become the Canadian capital of hotel chic, the W had its work cut out to impress with its own brand of high-fashion design. It succeeds in the rooms probably more than in the public spaces, though the glitterkittens in the Wunderbar late on in the evening probably don't notice. Ask for one of the irritatingly named Extreme Wow Suites (above), which have huge chaises longues/daybeds; deep, deep rectangular baths; lofty rainfall shower stalls; and faux-fur throws on the bed. It all just manages to stay on the good side of the Austin Powers shagpad aesthetic. The Whatever/Whenever button on the telephone brings you better-than-usual room and concierge service.

901 Square Victoria, T 514 395 3100, www.whotels.com

Hotel Gault

The most seriously design-conscious of Montreal's boutique hotels, the 30-room Gault shows off an embarrassment of midcentury classics in surroundings of polished concrete, steel and white oak. Owned by Montreal software magnate and arts benefactor Daniel Langlois, the former cotton warehouse in the heart of Old Montreal was sympathetically restored by local design duo Loukas Yiacouvakis and Marie-Claude Hamelin of Atelier YH2. The lobby, restaurant, bar and library are all housed in one open space, which acts as a gallery for Montreal's artists. The Top 5 rooms, such as Room 530 (above), have a contemporary loft feel, with a Bertoia chair or Artemide 'Tolomeo' lamp thrown in here and there.

449 rue Ste-Hélène, T 514 904 1616, www.hotelgault.com

Hotel Nelligan

The 63-room Nelligan manages to be cool, intimate and comfortable all at once. It occupies two buildings that date from the 1830s and has retained much exposed brick and stone. It has a Mediterranean-style Garden Atrium (above); contemporary suites with large bathrooms and swathes of rich fabric; and, on Thursdays in summer, its Rooftop SKY Terrace becomes one of the top spots in the city to preen and be seen. The best rooms are the Corner Deluxe Suites with their own fireplace and city views. The hotel is named after the 19th-century Quebecois poet Émile Nelligan, and its design is a collaboration between CDID Design and Montreal's CAMDI Design. *106 rue St-Paul Ouest, T 514 788 2040, www.hotelnelligan.com*

Hôtel Le Germain

In 1999, brothers Christiane and Jean-Yves Germain from Quebec City did their bit for the rejuvenation of Downtown by hiring Lemay Michaud Architecture Design to convert a 16-storey 1970s office block into a model of contemporary comfort, using an appealing combination of glass, dark wood, mirrors and high thread counts. In what was a novel move at the time, showers open onto the bedrooms, heightening the sense of space, but can be closed off with screens for privacy. The two luxury Bi-level Apartment Suites (Room 1603, above) are good value, while there is plenty more wood, concrete and light modern furniture in the public spaces, where the muscular, corporate feel of the original building blends in well with the modern detailing. *2050 rue Mansfield, T 514 849 2050, www.hotelgermain.com*

24 HOURS

SEE THE BEST OF THE CITY IN JUST ONE DAY

Montreal comes out top in all sorts of quality-of-life lists, because as well as having so many city-sized attractions, it is as deliciously easy to get around as your average small town. Traffic queues are laughably short to anyone used to New York or London, taxis are reasonable, public transport is plentiful and much of Montreal can be covered on foot. If you're feeling energetic, then hire a bike from Montreal On Wheels (27 rue de la Commune Est, T 514 866 0633), because, with more than 350km of cycle tracks and lanes, Montreal is the best city in North America to see on two wheels. We've taken advantage of this transport ease in plotting out a day that begins close to Old Montreal bordering Multimedia City, skirts around Mont-Royal to chichi Outremont and Mile End, and then passes through Downtown to the Centre Canadien d'Architecture (see p028) before finishing up back in Old Montreal.

The staggering levels of choice and quality among Montreal's restaurants have prompted us to include three full meals in the day, ending with dinner and dancing at Time Supper Club (see p030), where the beau monde come to party. To make up for this gastronomic overload, there are plenty of exercise options at the Parc du Mont-Royal, and if it's a Sunday, a chance to see the city's liberated, impromptu bongo-playing spirit at The Tamtams. In the US, such a display would attract baton-wielding policemen.

For full addresses, see Resources.

09.30 **Le Cartet**

Start your day's eating in a delightful old building on rue McGill, the road that divides post-industrial Multimedia City and Old Montreal. Le Cartet is a fine-food boutique and breakfast/brunch joint, delivering mammoth ham and egg platters, perfect pastries and takeaway treats. The original wooden floors and ramshackle tables, many of which are communal, encourage you to linger over *petit déjeuner*. At the

weekends, there is a mix of out-of-towners, on a break from cobblestone tourism, and the new generation of condo-dwellers who have colonised the surrounding streets of the old city. On weekdays, it is taken over by the designer-eyewear crowd on lunchbreak from the local digital offices.
106 rue McGill, T 514 871 8887

11.00 Mile End and Outremont

These two happening neighbourhoods are packed with design boutiques and up-to-the-minute architecture. Start your stroll on avenue Laurier Ouest at the upmarket kitchenware store Les Touilleurs (see p076) and the recent arrival Tampas Intérieurs (T 514 866 4145), which sells contemporary furniture as well as design classics. Next, head to Mile End, taking in the delightful Commissaires (see p073), before mooching around the furniture store Phil'z 20th Century Design (T 514 992 5190). Walk a few pleasant blocks across to 999 avenue McEachran to the Centre Communautaire Intergénérationnel (above), an award-winning community centre designed by Cardin+Ramirez. Its open-plan café (T 514 847 4100) is a handy place to rest.

13.30 Leméac

It's a short walk to this classic French bistro back on the distinctly bourgeois avenue Laurier Ouest. Leméac's deftly prepared, timeless dishes include a splendid lobster ravioli, but all the regular bistro faves are also on offer: steak frites, *boudin maison*, *pavé de foie de veau*, braised short rib and *cabillaud*. Architect Luc Laporte and owners Émile Saine and Richard Bastien have done a splendid job in creating a sleek, modern restaurant decked out in wood, mirrors and stainless steel. On sunny days, eat outside on the terrace. *1045 avenue Laurier Ouest, T 514 270 0999, www.restaurantlemeac.com*

16.00 Centre Canadien d'Architecture
The CCA boasts one of the world's largest collections of architectural documents, with around half a million items, including conceptual studies, plans, models and oral histories of individual architects. As a visitor, rather than a researcher, you're likely to be most interested in its rotating exhibitions and guided tours than its lectures, talks and study seminars. There are even family-based activities for those with a budding Le Corbusier in their midst. The CCA is based at Shaughnessy House, which was completed in 1874 and sympathetically added to in 1989. Across the highway, the gardens were designed by artist/architect Melvin Charney, and include a sculpture that is a full-size, partial mirror of Shaughnessy House.
1920 rue Baile, T 514 939 7026, www.cca.qc.ca

21.30 Time Supper Club

The supper club vibe is big in Montreal, and nowhere is it bigger and sexier than at Time. Enjoy a steak dinner and sample the tempting wine list in an atmosphere of undiluted glamour, boosted by the catwalk running through the restaurant. In summer, the action moves out to the rear terrace and its big white divans.
997 rue St-Jacques, T 514 392 9292, www.timesupperclub.com

URBAN LIFE
CAFÉS, RESTAURANTS, BARS AND NIGHTCLUBS

Once upon a time the cuisine most identified with Montreal was that of the Quebecois poor, such as *poutine* – fries, cheese curd and gravy – or a kind of pastrami called 'smoked meat'. But the French love of food has prevailed, with the added bonus of Italian, Jewish, Portuguese, Japanese and Vietnamese immigration and the riches of North American produce. Even in the economically lean times of the 1990s, chef/owners, such as Normand Laprise of <u>Toqué!</u> (see p042), created a contemporary local cuisine using ingredients from their bountiful countryside – and trained up a new generation of chefs whose restaurants now pepper the city. Today, competition keeps innovation as keen as kitchen knives, and the options run from classy and classic bistros, such as <u>Leméac</u> (see p027), to hip foodie destinations, such as <u>Garde Manger</u> (see p034) and Joe Beef (see p040), run by tattooed, rock'n'roll chefs.

Straightforward bars and nightclubs are fairly scarce at the top end – instead supperclub lounges are the big thing, where tables are cleared away at midnight so the DJ can start spinning. There are any number of velvet-rope hangouts for models and their pro ice-hockey-playing boyfriends to choose from on boulevard St-Laurent, where the cuisine is as good as the vibe. Montrealers know their food, they know their wine, they seem French and yet the service is friendly and attentive – so what's not to like?
For full addresses, see Resources.

Pullman

Local hotshot designer Bruno Braën is a regular at the cosy, stripped-back wine bar he has created in an otherwise quiet part of Downtown. The huge wine-glass chandelier is a fitting centrepiece to a bar with friendly, knowledgeable sommeliers, who serve more than 120 varietals by the glass from a staggeringly extensive cellar. Go for a selection of three tasting glasses, which are matched and sequenced by the house to maximise their impact on your taste buds. The modern tapas selection is not to be sniffed at, but the wine's the thing here. If you're in a group, head for the mezzanine floor – a splendid space to start off an evening. Pullman and Braën, who also designed Le Club Chasse et Pêche (see p048), were winners in the first Créativité Montréal awards in 2006. *3424 avenue du Parc, T 514 288 7779*

Garde Manger

Since opening in 2006, Garde Manger has managed to juggle a reputation for great seafood with a big following of beautiful people who make their way here to party late on Thursday and Friday nights. The fact that the place has quickly become a hangout for restaurant staff who've finished their shifts elsewhere speaks volumes. Chuck Hughes, the young and impressively tattooed co-owner and chef, formerly of Time Supper Club (see p030), decorated this former sailors' bar using a lot of junk that he found in the cellar. The best find of all was the wooden chandelier, all skulls and demons, rescued from an old Montreal theatre. If you would like to hear yourself speak, avoid Garde Manger at the weekend, but whenever you go, make sure two of you share the giant seafood platter as a starter.

408 rue St-François-Xavier, T 514 678 5044

Brontë
Accolades have brought the buzz without diminishing the quality of the food at Brontë. Its chef/owner Joe Mercuri creatively teams the best market-fresh ingredients — like foie gras and passion fruit — and presents them spectacularly. Book a buttercream leather booth for an amorous assignation.
1800 rue Sherbrooke Ouest, T 514 934 1801, www.bronterestaurant.com

Cluny ArtBar

A sort of workers' canteen for the loft-living artists and software designers who have clustered into the newly christened Multimedia City, the L-shaped Cluny ArtBar, which was designed by Jeremiah Gendron and Patrick Meausette, occupies a corner of the old Darling Brothers' foundry, which is now an art gallery. The beams in the ceiling, large metal-framed windows and very raw, unplastered brick walls have been left pretty much intact, and old bits of the foundry have been reused as coat hooks and the like. Dinner, served canteen-style on tables taken from an old bowling alley, is served only on Thursday evenings; the rest of the week join the buzzy lunch crowd for good-quality antipasti, *panini* and other fresh sandwiches.

257 rue Prince, T 514 866 1213,
www.cluny.info

Joe Beef

Fred Morin and David McMillan combine robust flavours, thousands of oysters and a name from history – the original Joe Beef was a Montreal canteen owner who gave free meals to the poor in return for work – to create one of the hottest gigs in town in up-and-coming Atwater. Book ahead or try at 9pm for a cancellation.
2491 rue Notre-Dame Ouest,
T 514 935 6504

Toqué!

Any list of Montreal's best restaurants usually places Normand Laprise's Toqué! at the top, and has done since it opened in 1993. His use of Quebecois ingredients, his partnerships with local producers and the chefs who have studied under him have made him one of the most important food figures in Canada. There were worries that moving to a bigger, more corporate space in the International Quarter would have an impact on his wild creativity, but the critics have decided everything is on track. Try the seven-course tasting menu: a range across the Quebec countryside chasing pigeon, stag, guinea fowl, scallops, morels, lobster and more. The décor, by Jean-Pierre Viau, is minimalist and muted. Closed on Sundays and Mondays.

900 place Jean-Paul-Riopelle, T 514 499 2084, www.restaurant-toque.com

Holts Café
The pared-down design is more hip bar
or art gallery than café, but it's the food
that makes Holts, in the basement of
premier department store Holt Renfrew,
such a hot lunchtime choice. Chef Corbin
Tomaszeski flies the Poilâne bread in
from Paris to create some of the most
wonderful sandwiches you'll ever taste.
1300 rue Sherbrooke Ouest,
T 514 842 5111, www.holtrenfrew.com

Olive et Gourmando

When chefs Dyan Solomon and Eric Girard left upscale eaterie Toqué! (see p042) in 1998 to set up their own coffee shop and bakery in the old city, they had a choice of several empty properties, so desolate was rue St-Paul Ouest. Now their splendid little café is the hub of a thriving district. At Olive et Gourmando, you'll find the best sourdough in the city, as well as the scrummiest cakes, brioches, croissants, sandwiches and tarts. The big windows and corner location make the café great for people-watching, and there are some interesting lampshades and other bits and bobs on sale. Linger over a coffee and rest up after pounding the cobbled streets. *351 rue St-Paul Ouest, T 514 350 1083, www.oliveetgourmando.com*

Le Club Chasse et Pêche
One of Montreal's true foodie delights.
Claude Pelletier and Hubert Marsolais
have created a short but innovative
menu focused on top-notch Canadian
ingredients and perfect delivery. The
warm, clubby interior by Bruno Braën
features photographs by Nicolas Baier
and kitsch lamps by Antoine Laverdière.
423 rue St-Claude, T 514 861 1112,
www.leclubchasseetpeche.com

Buonanotte

The party strip of Boulevard St-Laurent, or The Main, is dominated by Massimo Lecas and his associates, Roberto Pesut and Angelo Leone, who together own the glamour destinations Buonanotte, Time Supper Club (see p030), Time Boutique Café (T 514 842 2626), Globe Restaurant (T 514 284 3823) and foodie hangout Rosalie (T 514 392 1970). You would be hard-pressed to tell which attracts the best-looking crowd, especially during Formula One week, when all of them fill night after night with actresses, models, Saudi princes and racing drivers. Serving Italian cuisine in nightclub surroundings, Buonanotte probably just edges it on the question of which venue has had the highest number of waitresses hit on by a visiting Hollywood player.
3518 boulevard St-Laurent,
T 514 848 0644, www.buonanotte.com

Baldwin Barmacie

The cool, white, pharmacy-like décor of the Baldwin Barmacie is perfect for the part of avenue Laurier where it starts to change from ladies-who-lunch Outremont to lads-who-lounge Mile End. Owned by Alexandre Baldwin – formerly of the self-explanatory Whiskey Café (T 514 278 2646) and the hipster hangout GoGo Lounge (T 514 286 0882) – Barmacie is, apparently, a tribute to his grandmother, who worked in a local pharmacy (there's a nice picture on the website). Apart from an orange banquette, everything is white, off-white or beige, with the lower level given over to standing, perching or grooving. Hovering between inspired or ridiculous, depending on how many dirty martinis you've had, are the white leather chairs made from wine barrels and the adapted prison-issue loos in the ladies'.
115 avenue Laurier Ouest, T 514 276 4282, www.baldwinbarmacie.com

INSIDER'S GUIDE
BÉNÉDICTE PROUVOST, WRITER

Born in France, Bénédicte Prouvost is a writer for *Créativité Montréal* (www.creativitemontreal.com), the city's design and architecture publication, and for the graphic design journal *Grafika* (www.grafika.com). A resident of Plateau, her favourite restaurant is the sleek basement bistro Les Trois Petits Bouchons (4669 rue St-Denis, T 514 285 4444), where diners sit at one long blondwood table – great for a midweek supper with friends. The organic Quebec ingredients and modern French menu are particularly comforting on wintry Montreal evenings. For a more leisurely weekend lunch, she will head to Les Deux Singes de Montarvie (176 rue St-Viateur Ouest, T 514 278 6854) in Mile End, for its eclectic décor and welcoming staff.

Bar Plan B (327 avenue du Mont-Royal Est, T 514 845 6060), she says, is the place to go for an after-dinner nightcap, where 'despite the fact that it's usually packed, I like the décor – huge mirrors, cool seats – and the atmosphere is relaxed but classy'. For a more straightforward night out, she's a fan of the unpretentious vibe and vintage furnishings to be found at Baldwin Barmacie (see p052). Her favourite shops are the elegant bookstore Librissime (62 rue St-Paul Ouest, T 514 841 0123), where she hunts out texts on art, architecture, photography, travel and history, and the slice of design heaven that is Commissaires (see p073).

For full addresses, see Resources.

ARCHITOUR
A GUIDE TO MONTREAL'S ICONIC BUILDINGS

Montreal designers complain that Toronto, with its buildings by Gehry, Libeskind, Alsop, Lord Foster and Mayne, has 'bought' its built culture from elsewhere. The implication being that Montreal's architectural delights are more local and honest. In fact, many of its most notable buildings have been designed by international names. You can find pure corporate modernism by Mies van der Rohe and an experiment in modernist living by the Israeli/Canadian Moshe Safdie (see p066), as well as landmarks by IM Pei (see p012) and Buckminster Fuller (see p010). Many of these went up during Jean Drapeau's reign as mayor in the 1960s and 1970s, when the city was rebuilt and it hosted Expo 67 and the 1976 Olympics.

But even today, Montrealers continue to take their architecture seriously, and with two heralded architecture schools, as well as the research facility at the Centre Canadien d'Architecture (see p028), there is certainly no lack of knowledge. Important local architects include veterans Dan S Hanganu and Mario Saia, and more recently established stars such as Gilles Saucier, Michel Lapointe and the practice of Faucher Aubertin Brodeur Gauthier (FABG). Their contemporary work is rarely overtly showy; instead they take their cues from the geological folds of Mont-Royal, the grey-green of the roof tiles and granite in the city's older buildings and of Montreal's snow-filled winter skies.

For full addresses, see Resources.

TOHU

There are several architectural gems at the sprawling TOHU circus arts complex. It's here that the Cirque du Soleil has its Dan S Hanganu-designed international headquarters across the road from Canada's National Circus School, a steel-and-glass tower by Lapointe Magne et Associés, through whose windows you can see swinging trapeze artists. Built on an old landfill site, there is a strong eco ethic: the main performance space, the circular TOHU Pavilion (above), is reckoned to be the greenest building in Canada. Even the driveways are lined with vegetables, not corporate shrubs. We particularly like FABG's boxy circus artists' residence for the way that it references Habitat 67 (see p066).

St-Michel Environment Complex, 2345 rue Jarry Est, T 514 374 3522, www.tohu.ca

Olympic Stadium

Swooping and gorgeous it may be, but Roger Taillibert's Olympic Stadium went so colossally wrong it's hard to look at it without recalling Jean Drapeau's hostage-to-fortune quote: 'The Olympics can no more have a deficit than a man can have a baby.' Strikes meant the stadium wasn't finished in time for the 1976 games, and it wasn't until 1988 that the retractable roof worked; a later fixed roof collapsed and the main tenant, baseball team the Montreal Expos, left for Washington DC. The stadium eventually cost £810m, and not £67m as forecast. The attached velodrome is now a Biodome, although the Olympic Pool (see p090) is still in use. Ultimately, the arena isn't much more than a billion-dollar cable-car ride (one runs up the tower).
4141 avenue Pierre-de-Coubertin,
T 514 252 4737, www.rio.gouv.qc.ca

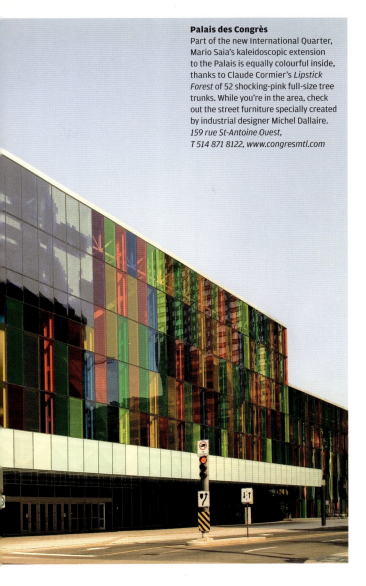

Palais des Congrès
Part of the new International Quarter,
Mario Saia's kaleidoscopic extension
to the Palais is equally colourful inside,
thanks to Claude Cormier's *Lipstick
Forest* of 52 shocking-pink full-size tree
trunks. While you're in the area, check
out the street furniture specially created
by industrial designer Michel Dallaire.
159 rue St-Antoine Ouest,
T 514 871 8122, www.congresmtl.com

Sun Life Building

A solid granite landmark, the Sun Life Building squats in the heart of Downtown, a symbol of the ups and downs of the city's economy over the past 90 years. When it was finished in 1933, it was the largest building in the British Empire and echoed the wealth that flowed out of Canada. During WWII, the British government dispatched its dwindling bullion reserves and the Crown Jewels to its steel-lined sub-basement. In the 1970s, however, Sun Life moved out, panicked, like so many other firms, by the upsurge of secessionist Quebecois politics. As Montreal's economy has recovered, so have the fortunes of the building, which is now home to the National Bank of Canada's futuristic trading floor, where plasma screens mix with original ornate features. *1155 rue Metcalfe*

Centre CDP Capital

Basically an office building perched on a bridge, the Centre CDP Capital is part of the International Quarter development. In the vast ocean-liner-like atrium, you can see the white steel columns that hold the building above the freeway below. High up in the lobby is a suspended square box, the Arbitrage Room, which playfully dangles in space and is packed with stock-exchange traders. The centre, designed by a consortium of architects that included FABG and Lemay Associés, links to the W Montreal hotel (see p020), the Palais des Congrès (see p060) and other newly spruced-up buildings. The fountain in the plaza outside, *La Joute* by Jean Paul Riopelle, is dramatically enveloped in mist and flames at set times each evening. *1000 place Jean-Paul-Riopelle, T 514 847 4100, www.centrecdpcapital.com*

Grande Bibliothèque du Quebec

Montreal's main library is a thoughtful piece of collaborative design that teams innovative materials with vast spaces and high-quality finishing. It was the work of three architecture practices: Gilles Guité, Croft Pelletier and Patkau Architects, who saw off 36 others in a competition to design the building. The exterior, clad in 6,000 plates of tempered, frosted glass, evokes the glacial green colour of Canada's far north landscape. Inside are two huge polished-concrete colonnaded areas, where native yellow birch is used in abundance to create screens that filter light and sound without closing off the spaces. The detailing, by design engineer Michel Dallaire, includes some funky, updated school reading desks.

475 boulevard de Maisonneuve Est,
T 514 873 1100, www.banq.qc.ca

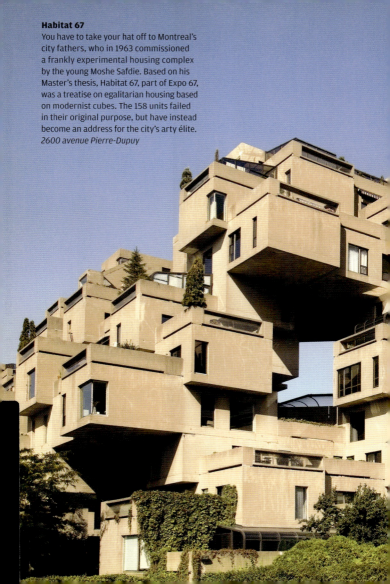

Habitat 67
You have to take your hat off to Montreal's city fathers, who in 1963 commissioned a frankly experimental housing complex by the young Moshe Safdie. Based on his Master's thesis, Habitat 67, part of Expo 67, was a treatise on egalitarian housing based on modernist cubes. The 158 units failed in their original purpose, but have instead become an address for the city's arty élite.
2600 avenue Pierre-Dupuy

L'ITHQ

A second skin of metal screens and
glass has transformed the once brutal
L'Institut de Tourisme et d'Hôtellerie du
Quebec. Lapointe Magne et Associés'
reworking fairly shimmers, changing in
the light and from different angles. The
interiors have also been injected with
a touch of glamour to ease students into
the city's increasingly chic hotel scene.
3535 rue St-Denis, ww.ithq.qc.ca

École de Musique Schulich
All sleek, thrusting horizontals, McGill
University's music building, designed by
Gilles Saucier and Anik Shooner, is one
of Downtown's most striking structures.
Windows puncture black cladding like
holes in a piano roll, Core-ten steel rusts
away nicely, and a concrete box houses
an acoustically perfect auditorium.
555 rue Sherbrooke Ouest,
T 514 398 4535, www.mcgill.ca

SHOPPING
THE BEST RETAIL THERAPY AND WHAT TO BUY

Montreal's main Downtown shopping strip, Ste-Catherine, could give London's Oxford Street a run for its money in the tacky and trashy stakes. Instead, head to distinct parts of the city for specific treats. There are a growing number of boutiques and speciality stores worth a look in Old Montreal, including the neat little multi-label designer store Reborn (231 rue St-Paul, T 514 499 8549), while the excellent bookstore Librissime (see p054) has a fine collection of tomes on art and architecture. At the other end of town, in Mile End, there are also boutiques, such as Commissaires (opposite), and cutting-edge designers, including Renata Morales (see p078), in a strip along boulevard St-Laurent. While in the area, you should definitely pay a visit to the St-Viateur Bagel Shop (263 rue St-Viateur Ouest, T 514 276 8044).

For other foods, there are Quebec cheeses and delicacies to be had at the city's markets, Atwater (see p013) to the west of the centre and Jean-Talon (7070 rue Henri-Julien, T 514 937 7754) in Little Italy. Meanwhile, a section of boulevard St-Laurent between rues Rachel and Mont-Royal is where the hip furniture stores cluster, including Interversion (4273 boulevard St-Laurent, T 514 284 2103), which specialises in Quebec-based designers, and the sofa stores Montauk (4404 boulevard St-Laurent, T 514 845 8285) and Moderno (4268 boulevard St-Laurent, T 514 842 4061).
For full addresses, see Resources.

Commissaires

At their lovely little gallery/boutique, Pierre Laramée and Josée Lapage have created a space that is quintessentially Montreal: diverse, high quality, amusing and relentlessly friendly and accessible. The pair select intelligently designed and sought-after items and curate them around themes that tell stories. You can find ceramics by Hella Jongerius, lighting by local architect Gilles Saucier and the Canadian duo Castor (above), £800, textiles, such as a wool and cotton plaid throw by Scholten & Baijings (above), £550, and chairs custom-made for the shop by Dutch designer Maarten Baas. There are also limited-edition pieces, such as Tobias Wong's 'McDonald's Coke Spoon' and crucifix brushes by FredriksonStallard. *5226 boulevard St-Laurent, T 514 274 4888, www.commissairesonline.com*

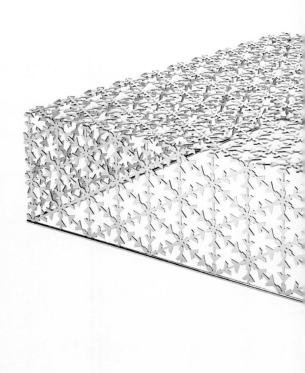

Periphere

This family design business is run by brother-and-sister team Thien and My Ta Trung, who have made something of a specialism of developing installations for chic hotels across North America and Air Canada's revamped VIP lounges. Unfortunately, they don't have a store, but you can pick up pieces from their collection at Interversion (see p072), the best place in town to seek out work from the hottest local furniture designers. We particularly like Periphere's 'Iceberg' table (above), £1,760. It was created from a sheet of steel that was laser-cut in order to create a repeating geometric snowflake pattern – it seems that in Montreal you can never really escape winter.

T 514 733 8588, www.periphere.com

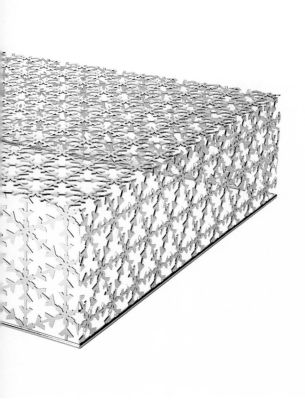

Les Touilleurs

Since it opened in 2002, Les Touilleurs has been the stylish gourmand's hangout of choice in upmarket Outremont. So much so that it had to double its floor space. It is a temple of kitchen design created by Louise Savoie, with all-white walls, large white display cabinets, long marble countertops and clever lighting. As well as looking good itself, it also sells some of the most stylish kitchenware in the business, including Wüsthof-Trident, All-Clad, Calphalon and Mauviel. Owners François Longré and Sylvain Côté also run cooking classes and chef demonstrations in the shop, for those who might actually want to get some of their stuff dirty.
152 avenue Laurier Ouest, T 514 278 0008, www.lestouilleurs.com

Renata Morales

The eclectic and avant-garde designer Renata Morales is an artist of some renown, who has become the darling designer of Montreal's indie music community. She relocated her boutique from Old Montreal to the more boho Mile End a couple of years ago and took over a studio, where she exhibits other artists' work. She uses her own art in textile designs, but also has shows of her paintings in galleries and other spaces. Her signature look started off as Mexican ruffles and high-collared blouses (she was born in Mexico), but she has since gone all over the fashion block. Her latest collections combine masculine and feminine pieces alongside bold 1960s graphic prints and Victorian whimsy.
5392 boulevard St-Laurent,
T 514 271 5061, www.renatamorales.com

Philippe Dubuc

Twice named Canadian Designer of the Year, Philippe Dubuc is a Montreal fashion institution, and has been producing slim, fitted menswear – always black, white, brown and shades in-between – since 1993. His equally crisp Gilles Saucier-designed boutique now sells womenswear upstairs. At one time, the Dubuc Mode de Vie label was sold in 80 stores worldwide and annual sales had hit the £1.5m mark.

However, being a high-end designer in a small market took its toll, and the cost of mounting shows, marketing and his exclusive use of local manufacturers forced Dubuc into bankruptcy in 2006. The wholesale arm has now gone, but thankfully this boutique was saved with the financial help of friends.
4451 rue St-Denis, T 514 282 1424, www.dubucstyle.com

WANT Les Essentiels de la Vie

How could we resist a line of luggage that comes with a pocket specifically designed to hold a Wallpaper* City Guide? WANT Les Essentiels de la Vie is a capsule collection of luxury travel accessories that includes overnight bags, the Trudeau laptop carrier (right), £310, and iPod wallets designed by Montreal twins Dexter and Byron Peart. The line is available locally from department store Holt Renfrew (T 514 842 5111), but the company has also started selling its pieces in Barneys New York, Fred Segal Finery in LA, Beams International Gallery in Tokyo and Harvey Nichols in London. The collection – each piece is named after an airport – is available in Italian leather or organic cotton from Turkey. There is also a range made in South Africa from crocodile and ostrich hide.
T 514 868 9268, www.wantessentiels.com

Marie Saint Pierre

An established figure in the Montreal fashion scene for more than 20 years, Marie Saint Pierre produces elegantly simple, yet stunningly sophisticated and versatile womenswear. Particularly perfect for frequent travellers is her collection of hand-textured taffeta, which looks better the more wrinkled it gets. When unpacked, many of her pieces can be transformed by being worn in a multitude of ways, from formal to casual: the four panels/ties of her classic white Kimono shirt can be tied in 25 different styles – including upside-down. Marie Saint Pierre's designs are sold throughout Canada and the US, but this industrial yet feminine-looking space in her native city is the showcase for her collection. Private shopping evenings are available for those wanting the personal touch.

2081 rue de la Montagne, T 514 281 5547, www.mariesaintpierre.com

Couleurs
In this small store/gallery, run by brothers
André and Lambert Gratton, you'll find
the city's best collection of Italian and
Scandinavian midcentury modern
classics. The shop also occasionally gets
hold of rarities by the likes of Canadian
furniture designer Russell Spanner and
jeweller Micheline de Passillé-Sylvestre.
3901 rue St-Denis, T 514 282 4141,
www.couleurs.qc.ca

Harricana

When Mariouche Gagné was a struggling fashion student in Milan, she entered a competition sponsored by the Fur Council of Canada. She didn't have the money for new materials, so she recycled her mother's old fur coat. And so a business idea was born. Her Harricana line brings the ethos of environmentalism to the otherwise unreconstructed world of the fur trade, recycling old coats into mittens, hats, vests, bags, cushions and rugs, and even kids' toys. While anti-fur campaigners would argue that she keeps demand for fur alive, Gagné's recycling programme claims that at least 500,000 fewer animals have been killed for the fur trade. Take along your granny's old coat and she will transform it and ship you the results.
3000 rue Ste-Antoine Ouest,
T 514 287 6517, www.harricana.qc.ca

SPORTS AND SPAS

WORK OUT, CHILL OUT OR JUST WATCH

With the exception of ice hockey, Montreal is not one of the world's great cities in which to be a sports fan. The owners of its Major League Baseball team, the Montreal Expos – named for Expo 67 – jumped ship after a history of small crowds, lamentable results and endless stadium problems. In 2005, the franchise moved to Washington DC to become the Washington Nationals. Typically, the team lost its last-ever home game 8-1, and the fans pelted the players with golf balls. The story of the Montreal Canadiens ice-hockey team is longer and more distinguished. Based at the Bell Centre (see p094) in Downtown, they were founded in 1909 and have won more Stanley Cups than any other team in the NHL. Unfortunately, the last time was in 1993, and there was a threat they would leave town too when they went up for sale in 2001. Probably the biggest spectator event of the year is the Canadian Grand Prix (opposite), which is inordinately popular, partly because the legendary Villeneuve motor-racing family come from just outside Montreal.

What the city does offer is plenty of exercise *en plein air*. You can cruise the Les Berges cycle path along the banks of the St Lawrence, or have fun on the river itself, by surfing, whitewater rafting or jet boating at the Lachine Rapids through Jet Boating Montreal (47 rue de la Commune Ouest, T 514 284 9607).
For full addresses, see Resources.

Circuit Gilles Villeneuve

Montrealers get ludicrously excited about the arrival of the Formula 1 Grand Prix every year, not so much because they are out-and-out petrol-heads, but because of the racing success of the Québécois Villeneuve family. The race takes place on the Île Notre-Dame, a man-made island on the St Lawrence created for Expo 67. The track was renamed after Gilles Villeneuve following his death in 1982 during practice laps for the Belgian Grand Prix. His son, Jacques, who was the 1997 F1 champion, owns a stylish supper club in town, Newtown (T 514 284 6555). The track is open all year round, even when there's no racing. It is used by cyclists, skaters and joggers, and connects with the Lachine Canal bike path.
Bassin Olympique, Île Notre-Dame, www.circuitgillesvilleneuve.ca

Olympic Park Sports Centre

Beneath Roger Taillibert's leaning tower lies the only part of the Olympic complex that is still regularly used for sport – its seven swimming pools. A great place for architecture fans who love to gaze at bare concrete while they do their laps, its swooping roof structure is supported on a series of piers. The ranks of empty seating can either be slightly spooky or play to your fantasies of being an Olympic swimmer in front of an imaginary crowd. Climb the diving boards for a scary leap into space. As you fall, consider Taillibert's response to those (the whole city) who complained about the cost of his vision: 'There are always critics – only those who do nothing have no critics.' Call for opening times, as it often closes for competitions. *3200 rue Viau, T 514 252 4622, www.rio.gouv.qc.ca*

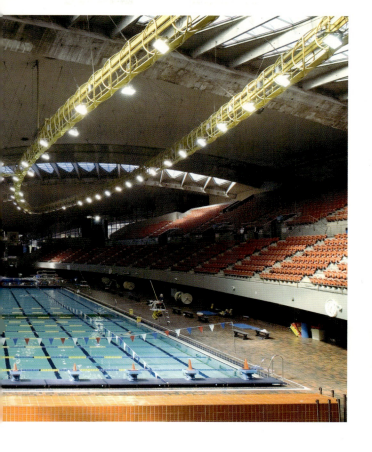

Away Spa at W Montreal
Once upon a time, the hirsute gentleman
had to rely on a discreet nod to his barber
to keep his eyebrows in check. These days
there's Brow Grooming at the Away Spa,
which offers special male packages, as
well as many treatments for women, in
a minimalist Japanese-style space filled
with sliding doors and lotus flowers.
901 Square Victoria, T 514 395 3160,
www.starwoodhotels.com

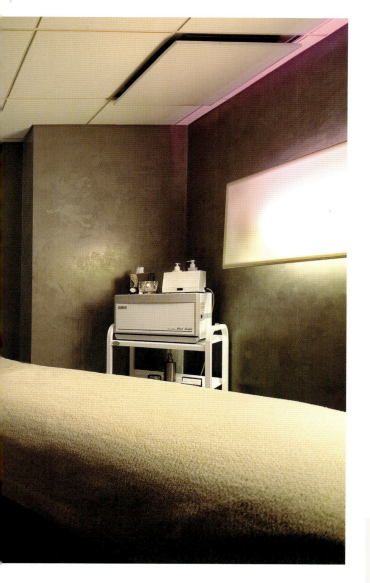

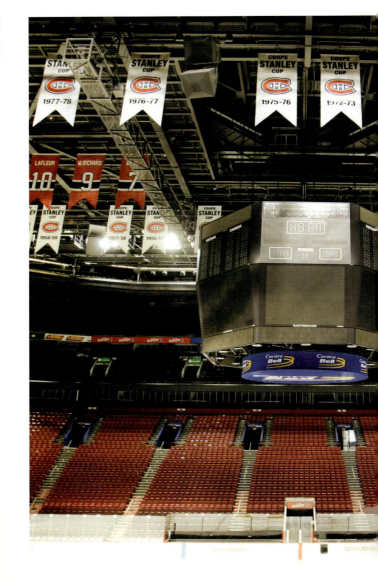

Speedpass

Bell Centre

Hardly an architectural gem from the outside, the Bell Centre is dramatically vertiginous on the inside. The Montreal Canadiens moved here in 1996 from their historic old home, the Montreal Forum, where they had won more Stanley Cup hockey championships than any other team. At the Bell Centre, known first as the Molson Centre after the club's previous owners, to date they have won precisely zip. The venue includes an amphitheatre, theatre and a hemicycle seating area; the total seating capacity is 21,500, when part of the ice rink is used to accommodate spectators. This place is where you'll find all the major stadium rock acts as they pass through town. For devoted fans of ice hockey, there is also a cavernous bar/ restaurant filled with obscure memorabilia. *1260 rue de la Gauchetière Ouest, T 514 790 1245, www.bellcentre.ca*

ESCAPES

WHERE TO GO IF YOU WANT TO LEAVE TOWN

It doesn't take long to get out of Montreal and into the ravishing Quebec countryside. The province is big – three times the size of France – and extremely beautiful. It's chiefly made up of the populous St Lawrence river valley, farmland and a wilderness that stretches all the way north to Hudson Bay and the Arctic; a landscape of rivers, mountains and lakes, with a population dominated by native North American caribou and fish.

If time is an issue, you can stay relatively close to Montreal and still explore wild destinations. Just to the north of the city are the Laurentians, an extension of the Adirondack Mountains in New York State, and to the east are the Appalachian Mountains, which reach into the Eastern Townships region near the border with the US. In both ranges, you will find a particularly Quebecoise type of tourism – excellent cuisine and luxurious comfort combined with outstanding natural beauty. You could also rouse yourself from self-indulgence and get active: there is world-class whitewater rafting to be had on the Rouge River (New World Rafting, Place St-Bernard, T 819 242 7238), or you could go skiing in Mont-Tremblant (see p100), eastern Canada's answer to Whistler. But if you just want to chill out, we've found an exquisite designer spa (see p102) hidden in a wildlife reserve by a lake. Its attractions include waterfalls and a natural bathing pond.

For full addresses, see Resources.

Quebec City

Just two and a half hours away, Montreal's smaller, more innocent neighbour has a heart that is all French. The old Upper Town was built on palisades above the St Lawrence to avoid fire from the British, and its nest of slate-roofed buildings is probably more peachy perfect than any French town from the 18th century. The Lower Town was once all wharves, warehouses and heavy industry, but increasing numbers of shops, cafés and bars have opened up. Find time to admire the interior of Moshe Safdie's Musée de la Civilisation (overleaf; T 418 643 2158), while on the accommodation front, sumptuous Auberge St-Antoine (T 418 692 2211) or new boutique Hotel 71 (T 418 692 1171), in an old bank building, are the best options.

Entrance hall, Musée de la Civilisation, Quebec City

Hôtel Quintessence, Mont-Tremblant

The fabulous, swanky ski resort of Mont-Tremblant, just 80km outside Montreal, hasn't been entirely despoiled by the Range Rover-driving, fur-wearing classes. Instead, it has managed to retain plenty of serenity, thanks to its stunning location at the southern tip of Lake Tremblant and below the eponymous mountain. It is surrounded by quiet woods and yet the town itself has the air of a small, smart city. Out of the ski season, there is more than enough to keep you occupied on the lake, and there's also hiking in the woods. The pick of places to stay in town is Hôtel Quintessence (above), a 30-suite boutique hotel with a classy hunting-lodge feel. Every room has a wood-burning fireplace and a private terrace overlooking the lake. *3004 Chemin de la Chapelle, T 819 425 3400, www.hotelquintessence.com*

Balnea Spa, Bromont-sur-le-Lac
About an hour's drive from Montreal,
Balnea Spa is a destination in its own
right – one that comes complete with
lashings of cool, contemporary design
and an unbeatable location by a lake in
the middle of a private nature reserve.
Facilities include outdoor whirlpools and
Finnish saunas with panoramic views.
319 chemin du Lac Gale, T 450 534 0604,
www.balnea.ca

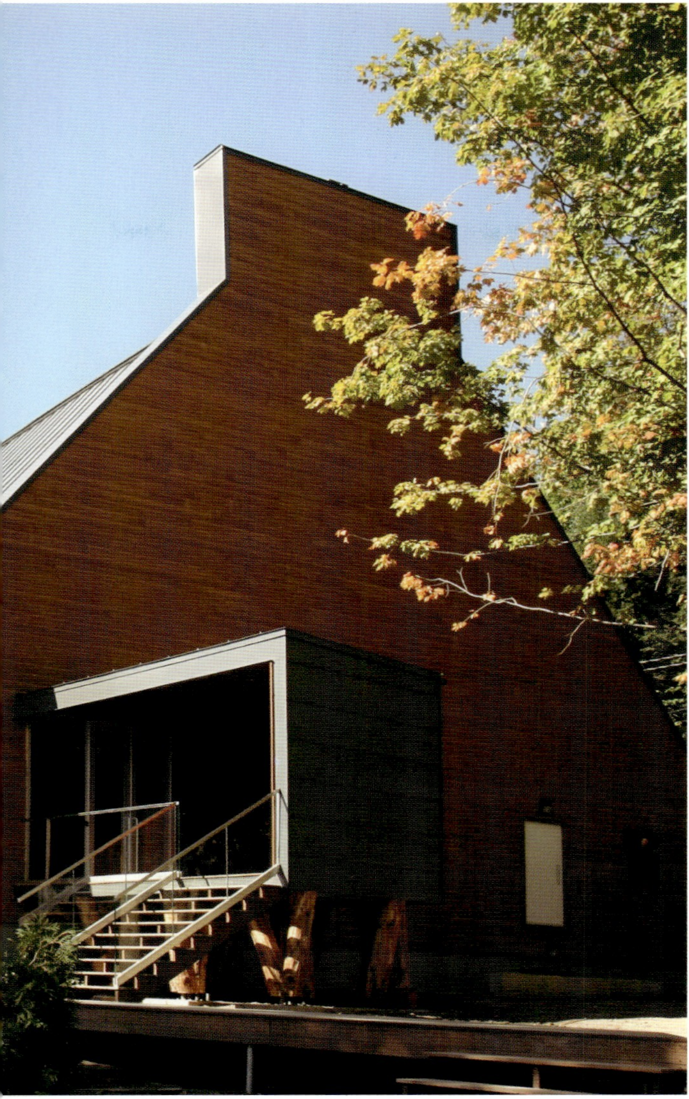

NOTES

SKETCHES AND MEMOS

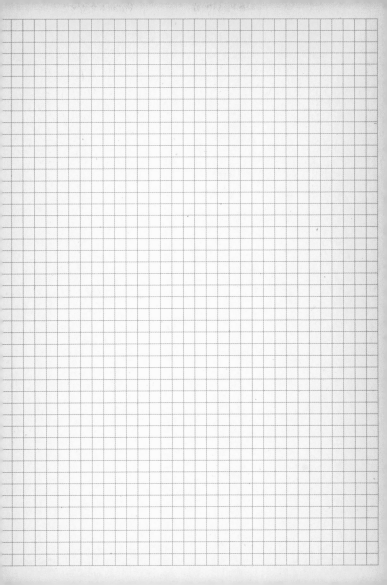

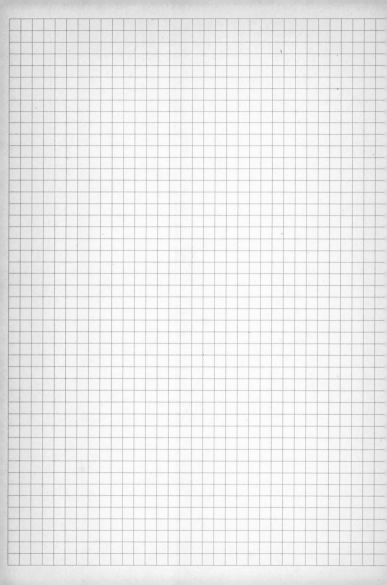

RESOURCES

CITY GUIDE DIRECTORY

A

Atwater Market 013
138 avenue Atwater
T 514 937 7754
www.marchespublics-mtl.com
Away Spa at W Montreal 092
901 Square Victoria
T 514 395 3160
www.starwoodhotels.com

B

Baldwin Barmacie 052
115 avenue Laurier Ouest
T 514 276 4282
www.baldwinbarmacie.com
Balnea Spa 102
319 chemin du Lac Gale
Bromont-sur-le-Lac
T 450 534 0604
www.balnea.ca
Bar Plan B 054
327 avenue du Mont-Royal Est
T 514 845 6060
www.barplanb.ca
Bell Centre 094
1260 rue de la Gauchetière Ouest
T 514 790 1245
www.bellcentre.ca
Biosphère 010
160 chemin Tour-de-l'Isle
Île Ste-Hélène
T 514 283 5000
www.biosphere.ec.gc.ca
Brontë 036
1800 rue Sherbrooke Ouest
T 514 934 1801
www.bronterestaurant.com
Buonanotte 050
3518 boulevard St-Laurent
T 514 848 0644
www.buonanotte.com

C

Le Cartet 025
106 rue McGill
T 514 871 8887
**Centre Canadien
d'Architecture** 028
1920 rue Baile
T 514 939 7026
www.cca.qc.ca
Centre CDP Capital 063
1000 place Jean-Paul-Riopelle
T 514 847 4100
www.centrecdpcapital.com
**Centre Communautaire
Intergénérationnel** 026
999 avenue McEachran
T 514 847 4100
Circuit Gilles Villeneuve 089
Bassin Olympique
Île Notre-Dame
www.circuitgillesvilleneuve.ca
Le Club Chasse et Pêche 048
423 rue St-Claude
T 514 861 1112
www.leclubchasseetpeche.com
Cluny ArtBar 038
257 rue Prince
T 514 866 1213
www.cluny.info
Commissaires 073
5226 boulevard St-Laurent
T 514 274 4888
www.commissaliresonline.com
Couleurs 084
3901 rue St-Denis
T 514 282 4141
www.coleurs.qc.ca

HOTELS

ADDRESSES AND ROOM RATES

Auberge St-Antoine 097
Room rates:
double, from C$160
8 rue St-Antoine
Quebec City
T 418 692 2211
www.st-antoine.com

Fairmont The Queen Elizabeth 016
Room rates:
double, C$220
900 boulevard Réne-Lévesque Ouest
T 514 861 3511
www.fairmont.com/queenelizabeth.com

Hotel Gault 021
Room rates:
double, from C$210;
Room 530, C$650
449 rue Ste-Hélène
T 514 904 1616
www.hotelgault.com

Hôtel Le Germain 023
Room rates:
double, C$400;
Bi-level Apartment Suite, from C$950
2050 rue Mansfield
T 514 849 2050
www.hotelgermain.com

Hotel Nelligan 022
Room rates:
double, C$235;
Corner Deluxe Suite, C$390
106 rue St-Paul Ouest
T 514 788 2040
www.hotelnelligan.com

Hôtel Quintessence 100
Room rates:
suite, from C$300
3004 Chemin de la Chapelle
Mont-Tremblant
T 819 425 3400
www.hotelquintessence.com

The Ritz-Carlton 016
Room rates:
double, from C$130
1228 rue Sherbrooke Ouest
T 514 842 4212
www.ritzmontreal.com

Hotel 71 097
Room rates:
double, from C$165
71 rue St-Pierre
Quebec City
T 418 692 1171
www.hotel71.ca

Sofitel 017
Room rates:
double, from C$145;
suite, from C$235
1155 rue Sherbrooke Ouest
T 514 285 9000
www.sofitel.com

Hôtel St-Paul 018
Room rates:
double, C$280;
Deluxe Suite, C$370;
Penthouse Junior Suite 1005, C$390
355 rue McGill
T 514 380 2222
www.hotelstpaul.com

W Montreal 020
Room rates:
double, from C$300;
Extreme Wow Suite, from C$2,500
901 Square Victoria
T 514 395 3100
www.whotels.com

WALLPAPER* CITY GUIDES

Editorial Director
Richard Cook

Art Director
Loran Stosskopf
City Editor
Paul McCann
Editor
Rachael Moloney
**Executive
Managing Editor**
Jessica Firmin
Travel Bookings Editor
Sara Henrichs

Chief Designer
Daniel Shrimpton
Designer
Lara Collins
Map Illustrator
Russell Bell

Photography Editor
Christopher Lands
Photography Assistant
Robin Key

Chief Sub-Editor
Jeremy Case
Sub-Editors
Vicky McGinlay
Melanie Wells
Assistant Sub-Editor
Milly Nolan
Editorial Assistant
Ella Marshall

**Wallpaper* Group
Editor-in-Chief**
Tony Chambers
Publisher
Neil Sumner

Contributors
Lynda Brault
Meirion Pritchard
Ellie Stathaki

Wallpaper* ® is a
registered trademark
of IPC Media Limited

All prices are correct at
time of going to press,
but are subject to change.

PHAIDON

Phaidon Press Limited
Regent's Wharf
All Saints Street
London N1 9PA

Phaidon Press Inc
180 Varick Street
New York, NY 10014

Phaidon® is a registered
trademark of Phaidon
Press Limited

www.phaidon.com

First published 2008
© 2008 IPC Media Limited

ISBN 978 0 7148 4747 4

A CIP Catalogue record for
this book is available from
the British Library.

Printed in China

PHOTOGRAPHERS

MONTREAL
A COLOUR-CODED GUIDE TO THE HOT 'HOODS

PLATEAU
One of the city's most desirable districts is replete with French bistros and swanky clubs

MULTIMEDIA CITY
Galleries and cafés nestle in between waterfront warehouses and contemporary offices

OUTREMONT
Visit this popular Francophone enclave for upscale shopping and leisurely lunches

DOWNTOWN
Home to the design-led International Quarter, department stores and an underground city

GAY VILLAGE
The self-proclaimed biggest gay village in North America is a riot of colour and cool

MILE END
Mix with artists and designers in the bars and boutiques of this boho neighbourhood

OLD MONTREAL
The previously neglected old city centre now boasts classy hotels, shops and restaurants

LATIN QUARTER
This entertainment zone comes alive in summer, hosting a succession of outdoor festivals

For a full description of each neighbourhood, see the Introduction.
Featured venues are colour-coded, according to the district in which they are located.